HOLY**HABITS** | MISSIONAL DISCIPLESHIP RESOURCES FOR CHURCHES

The Bible Reading Fellowship
15 The Chambers, Vineyard
Abingdon OX14 3FE
brf.org.uk

The Bible Reading Fellowship (BRF) is a Registered Charity (233280)

ISBN 978 0 85746 686 0
First published 2018
10 9 8 7 6 5 4 3 2 1 0
All rights reserved

Acknowledgements
Unless otherwise acknowledged, scripture quotations from The New Revised Standard Version of the Bible, Anglicised edition, copyright © 1989, 1995 by the Division of Christian Education of the National Council of the churches of Christ in the United States of America. Used by permission. All rights reserved.

Scripture quotations on cover and title page, or marked NIV, are taken from The Holy Bible, New International Version (Anglicised edition) copyright © 1979, 1984, 2011 by Biblica. Used by permission of Hodder & Stoughton Publishers, a Hachette UK company. All rights reserved. 'NIV' is a registered trademark of Biblica. UK trademark number 1448790.

Photographs on pages 33 and 53 copyright © Thinkstock; photographs on pages 4, 13, 23, 27, 42, 44, 46 and 61 copyright © Tom Milton and the Birmingham Methodist Circuit.

Every effort has been made to trace and contact copyright owners for material used in this resource. We apologise for any inadvertent omissions or errors, and would ask those concerned to contact us so that full acknowledgement can be made in the future.

A catalogue record for this book is available from the British Library

Printed and bound by CPI Group (UK) Ltd, Croydon CR0 4YY

CONTENTS

To order more copies of the Holy Habits resources, or to find out
how to download pages for printing or projection on screen,
please visit brfonline.org.uk/holy-habits.

Remember the context

This Holy Habit is set in the context of ten Holy Habits, and the ongoing life of your church and community.

> They devoted themselves to the apostles' teaching and fellowship, to the breaking of bread and the prayers. Awe came upon everyone, because many wonders and signs were being done by the apostles. All who believed were together and had all things in common; they would sell their possessions and goods and distribute the proceeds to all, as any had need. Day by day, as they spent much time together in the temple, they broke bread at home and ate their food with glad and generous hearts, **praising God** and having the goodwill of all the people. And day by day the Lord added to their number those who were being saved.
> ACTS 2:42–47

A prayer for the faithful practice of Holy Habits

This prayer starts with a passage from Romans 5:4–5.

Endurance produces character, and character produces hope,
and hope does not disappoint us...
Gracious and ever-loving God, we offer our lives to you.
Help us always to be open to your Spirit in our thoughts
and feelings and actions.
Support us as we seek to learn more about those habits of the Christian life
which, as we practise them, will form in us the character of Jesus
by establishing us in the way of faith, hope and love.
Amen

INTRODUCTION

Worship features prominently in Luke's writings. He presents people praising God in response to experiencing God's loving help or saving grace (Luke 2:13, 20; 19:37; Acts 3:8, etc.). Praise and **Worship** flow from gratitude for who God is and what God has done. The first story he tells is set in the context of **Worship**. Zechariah receives the news that his prayers have been heard and that he and Elizabeth are to have a son (Luke 1:5–13). His Gospel concludes with Jesus' ascension and the disciples **Worshipping** him before returning to Jerusalem where 'they were continually in the temple blessing God' (Luke 24:53). When Acts unfurls, **Worship** is at the heart of the early church. Spirit-filled, exuberant praise offered in the home, the temple and on the streets.

There is a risk that we think of **Worship** only as something that happens when Christians gather for an hour or two. While gatherings are a habit to be encouraged, there is much more to **Worship** than this. **Worship** is a way of life, one encapsulated in the Jewish Shema: a prayer which is the centre piece of Jewish morning and evening prayer services. It includes these words from Deuteronomy 6:5:

> Love the Lord your God with all your heart, and with all your soul, and with all your might.

Worship offered as grateful response involves all of our lives; our work, rest, enjoyment of creation, service, eating, giving – and, yes, our gatherings for the focused activity of services of **Worship**. Tending the crops, forming an algorithm, building a house or serving a customer can all be done as acts of **Worship** to the glory of God, as can the singing of songs, the offering of dance, sculpture or art and the praying of prayers.

	Resources particularly suitable for children and families
	Resources particularly suitable for young people
CH4	Church Hymnary 4 (also known as Hymns of Glory Songs of Praise)
RS	Rejoice and Sing
SoF	Songs of Fellowship 6
StF	Singing the Faith

Reflections

There are times when **Worship** is instinctive and obvious – when we have such a sense of deep joy that we cannot help but worship God. And there are times in life when the last thing we feel like doing is worshipping God.

The Psalms offer a lovely example: honest and open with God in good times and bad; whether moaning or praising, always in touch with God. In many psalms, the psalmist is clearly excited about God and wanting to praise God with every part of their being. They also regularly recount troubles and moans, and tell God what to do. In Psalms 42 and 43, the psalmist shares difficulties with God but, despite everything, trusts, hopes and praises. This is not because the psalmist feels like it, but because God deserves praise – because God is God regardless of circumstances. So, because God is God, the psalmist knows there is hope.

Worship can arise from a glad heart, but it can also be the deliberate choice of a hurting one. All of life can be **Worship** when lived for love of God. So, resourcing for **Worship**, learning to **Worship** even when we don't feel like it, learning to make everything we do in our daily lives a **Worship** offering to God, is about 24/7, everyday discipleship.

In exploring this Holy Habit, we pray you will discover more of God; we hope that you will be able to have conversations which help deepen your relationships with God and with each other as you build lives which **Worship** God.

UNDERSTANDING THE HABIT

WORSHIP RESOURCES

Below are some thoughts and ideas for how you might incorporate this Holy Habit into acts of **Worship**.

Biblical material

Old Testament passages:

- Deuteronomy 6:1–9   Love the Lord your God
- Psalm 8   Divine majesty and human dignity
- Psalm 96   Sing to the Lord a new song
- Psalm 100   A psalm of thanksgiving
- Isaiah 6:1–8   Heavenly worship
- Amos 5:18–24   The kind of worship God desires
- Habakkuk 3   Habakkuk's prayer

Gospel passages:

- Matthew 6:1–21   How we worship
- Matthew 28:1–10, 16–20   The resurrection and great commission
- Luke 2:25–38   Jesus is presented in the temple
- John 4:19–24   True worship

Other New Testament passages:

- Acts 16:16–34   Paul and Silas in prison
- Romans 12   A living sacrifice
- Ephesians 2:1–10   Made alive with Christ
- Revelation 5:6–14   The Lamb opens the scroll

Suggested hymns and songs

When we think about **Worship**, our thoughts might naturally turn first to our favourite worship songs or hymns. However, singing and music are of course only part of **Worship**. Given that this habit is intended to challenge you to a deeper exploration of **Worship**, consider choosing hymns or songs you are less familiar with. Consider how different songs can be used to help us in different aspects of our **Worship**, such as confession, offering or petition – as well as praise, thankfulness and adoration. How does it feel to read a song out loud instead of singing it? Or to really sing out a song of praise to God when you are truly alone with God? If you are musical, how does it feel to compose a piece of music purely for your individual praise of God?

- As we are gathered Jesus is here (CH4 197, RS 469)
- Be still and know that I am God (CH4 754/755, RS 347, StF 18)
- Beyond these walls of worship (StF 547)
- Born in song (StF 21)
- Calm me, Lord, as you calmed the storm (StF 624)
- Come, let us join our cheerful songs (RS 382, StF 743)
- Come O Lord, give us your Spirit (StF 759)
- Come, now is the time to worship (CH4 196, StF 24)
- Endless hallelujah (When I stand before your throne) ☺
- Eternal God, your love's tremendous glory (RS 33, StF 3)
- Father, we praise you, now the night is over (CH4 209, RS 33)
- Fill thou my life, O Lord my God (CH4 183, RS 406, StF 73)
- From glory to glory advancing (RS 462)
- Give me joy in my heart, keep me praising (StF 76)
- Glory to God, glory to God (CH4 760 and 762, RS 8, StF 753)
- God be in my head (CH4 538, RS 498)
- God is unique and one (RS 35)
- Great is thy faithfulness, O God my Father (CH4 153, RS 96, StF 51)
- How shall I sing that majesty (CH4 128, RS 661, StF 53)
- I will offer up my life (CH4 503, StF 446)
- I will worship (StF 54)
- In the Lord I'll be ever thankful (CH4 772, StF 776)
- Jesu, tawo pano (CH4 773, StF 27)
- King of glory, King of peace (RS 97, StF 56)
- Light of the world (RS 504, StF 175)
- Lord of creation, to you be all praise (CH4 500, RS 532, StF 449)
- Nothing in all creation (RS 397)
- O worship the Lord in the beauty of holiness (StF 34)
- Take, oh take me as I am (CH4 795, StF 781)

- The peace of the earth be with you (CH4 798, StF 774)
- There's a quiet understanding (RS 412, StF 36)
- This, this is the God we adore (StF 67)
- To God be the glory, great things he has done (CH4 512, RS 289, StF 94)
- What of those Sabbaths? (RS 659)
- When in our music God is glorified (RS 414, StF 731)
- When the music fades (StF 437) ☺
- With gladness we worship (StF 17)
- With joyful lips we sing to you (CH4 671)
- Worship the Lord in the beauty of holiness (CH4 201, RS 187, StF 34)

Introduction to the theme 👪

Prepare four or five 'smelly' things in containers, presented on a table for all to see. This could include vinegar, a fragranced candle, some expensive perfume or aftershave (sprayed on a card so it's not easily identifiable from its bottle), a piece of blue cheese, crisps or fabric softener. They could be hidden and revealed one at a time, for example under boxes or a cloth.

Also prepare postcards, a large sheet of paper (a roll of lining paper or a paper tablecloth would work well) with 'Wow!' printed or written on, felt-tip pens, a bottle of bubble bath, a plastic sheet or large tray and some cloths or kitchen roll for cleaning up. You may also want a can of air freshener for afterwards!

Open the time by stating that we place value on different things – depending on what we believe they're worth, how rare they are or how much they mean to us. Ask if we might be able to place the following things in their order of worth or which has the lowest/highest value.

Invite a couple of members of the congregation to participate and smell each item, then place them in the order they value them. Follow this by spraying some air freshener around the room, seeing how it fills the space with its fragrance. Talk about how our actions, attitudes, behaviour and words can make a difference to those around us. Offering praise or **Worship** to God changes the atmosphere of our situations.

Explain the close relationship between the words 'worship' and 'worth-ship', and that the latter helps us better understand what **Worship** is really all about. Sometimes we might assume it simply describes how we use music to praise God, but it's so much more than that! It's about how we express our awe and wonder of who God is in a million different ways. Invite the congregation to recall a time they said 'Wow!' out loud on experiencing something amazing. (You may wish to ask for a few of these to be shared.) Alternatively, put the word 'Wow!' on to postcards or a large sheet of paper and encourage everyone to draw or write their moment on it. Add that when we encounter something or someone amazing, our response is important – it's rare that we would feel the need to do nothing!

In Matthew 26:6–13, a woman arrives while Jesus is eating with friends and does something extraordinary. To demonstrate, invite a volunteer to stand with their hands cupped in front of them – pour a whole bottle of bubble bath over their hands (protect the surrounding area!). Make a display of using every last drop of the liquid. It seems extravagant – that's exactly what Jesus' friends thought too, but the woman wanted to demonstrate just how important he was to her, how much he was worth, so it was an act of her 'worth-ship' to use such expensive perfume. Jesus was much more precious to her than the fragrance. I wonder what we might want to give as our **Worship**?

Talk about some ideas with the person next to you or in small groups. Take some suggestions. Invite the congregation to shout out one word that describes the awesomeness of God on the count of three... (Feel free to repeat this if there is enthusiasm!)

Close this time by praying and thanking God for who he is – alternatively, invite one or two to do this on behalf of everyone.

Thoughts for sermon preparation

Hebrews 8:1–7, John 4:23–24

Now the main point in what we are saying is this: we have such a high priest, one who is seated at the right hand of the throne of the Majesty in the heavens, a minister in the sanctuary and the true tent [or tabernacle] that the Lord, and not any mortal, has set up. For every high priest is appointed to offer gifts and sacrifices; hence it is necessary for this priest also to have something to offer. Now if he were on earth, he would not be a priest at all, since there are priests who offer gifts according to the law. They offer worship in a sanctuary that is a sketch and shadow of the heavenly one; for Moses, when he was about to erect the tent, was warned, 'See that you make everything according to the pattern that was shown you on the mountain.' But Jesus has now obtained a more excellent ministry, and to that degree he is the mediator of a better covenant, which has been enacted through better promises.

HEBREWS 8:1–7

But the hour is coming, and is now here, when the true worshippers will worship the Father in spirit and truth, for the Father seeks such as these to worship him. God is Spirit, and those who worship him must worship in spirit and truth.

JOHN 4:23–24

These sermon thoughts focus particularly on the reading from Hebrews 8 and Jesus' interaction with the Samaritan woman in John 4. The letter to the Hebrews has the purpose of bridging the New and Old Covenants, so it is important to make reference also to Old Testament passages. Good examples to draw on are:

- Isaiah 1:11–18   God's disgust at the **Worship** of an unrighteous people
- Micah 6:6–8   **Worship** and what God requires
- Isaiah 6:1–8   **Worship** in heaven

The following psalms might be helpful in supporting the themes in these scripture passages:

- Psalm 24
- Psalm 30
- Psalm 33
- Psalm 42
- Psalm 51 (vv. 1–2, 15–17)
- Psalm 66 (vv. 1–4)
- Psalm 92 (vv. 1–4)
- Psalm 95 (vv. 1–7)
- Psalm 98
- Psalm 100
- Psalm 148
- Psalm 150

You might wish to refer also to other New Testament passages:

- James 1:27   True religion (note how this verse echoes Isaiah 1:17)
- Revelation 1:12–18   A vision of the glorified Christ (note the parallel with Isaiah 6:6–8)

Some thoughts on major themes which can be reflected on in a sermon include the following:

Awe and wonder are appropriate responses to God's beauty and glory. Sometimes it is said that God demands our worship in the same sense that a great work of art or a scene of natural beauty demands our appreciation.

Expressions of **Worship** can include prayers of praise, singing or actions like kneeling, raising hands, or even falling on our faces if we are truly struck with awe, like John in Revelation 1. But in order to **Worship** 'in spirit and truth', our words and gestures must be motivated by the right intentions, not just as a matter of 'going through the motions' or trying to flatter God. It is important to note that it is intention, not feelings, that matter. We can be tired or distracted or even troubled by feelings that our motives are mixed, but we can still choose to place ourselves intentionally before God with the intention to **Worship** and ask that God's grace carries us when, sometimes, it may not feel as if we even desire to **Worship**.

But right intentions also imply an active commitment on our part to do what we can do. Reflect on Isaiah's prophesying against the **Worship** of the people in chapter 1: they intentionally chose to do what was wrong in the eyes of God, and then thought that they could win the approval of God by their overt acts of worship, worship which was not offered in spirit and in truth. Refer to Isaiah 1:17 and James 1:27 on true religion.

Notice that although the letter to the Hebrews (10:4) says that 'it is impossible for the blood of bulls and goats to take away sins', these are not condemned *in themselves*. Any act which is done with right intentions, and arising from love, can be a valid way of **Worshipping** God. That is where the people whom Isaiah condemns fell short. But what the letter to the Hebrews does say is that these acts are 'only a shadow of the good things to come and not the true form of these realities' (10:1). This understanding had already developed in the Old Testament, as we see in Psalm 51:17: 'The sacrifice acceptable to God is a broken spirit; a broken and contrite heart, O God, you will not despise'; or, as the alternative NRSV reading of Psalm 50:14 says, 'Make thanksgiving your sacrifice to God'.

Something must also be said about places of **Worship**. In Jesus' conversation with the Samaritan women, he tells her, 'The hour is coming when you will **Worship** the Father neither on this mountain [Mount Gerizim, where the Samaritan temple was] nor in Jerusalem.' We can see in this Jesus' further development of the idea of the deeper truth of **Worship**, which we see in the verses of Psalms 50 and 51 we have just read. For Christians, the whole earth can be regarded as God's temple – the place where God dwells. Similarly, Paul asks the Christians in Corinth about sin against their bodies: 'Or do you not know that your body is a temple of the Holy Spirit within you?' (1 Corinthians 6:19), and goes on to tell them to glorify God in their bodies (6:20). Treating and using our bodies in a way that honours their Creator is a way of **Worshipping** him.

None of this disqualifies us from coming together in corporate **Worship** as Christians have done for two millennia, but it does put **Worship** into perspective.

Prayers

A responsive prayer of praise

When life is good and my heart feels glad
I will praise you, beautiful God

When life is dull and every day feels the same
I will praise you, beautiful God

When I feel hopeful and life is falling into place perfectly
I will praise you, beautiful God

When I feel no hope for the future and I can't see a way forward
I will praise you, beautiful God

When life is wonderful and those I love are thriving
I will praise you, beautiful God

When I get wrapped up in myself and my own concerns
I will praise you, beautiful God

When I get overwhelmed with the world and all the need
I will praise you, beautiful God

Because I am your friend and disciple, because I know your heart
I will praise you, beautiful God

Whatever the circumstance, because of you who are
I will praise you, beautiful God
I will praise you, beautiful God

A prayer of adoration 👪

Dear God,
You are the most awesome God. And you are very worthy and we are unworthy
to let you serve us.
Amen

An intercessory prayer of worship

Creator God,

We look around and see the beauty of your world,
the backdrop of colour enhancing the sights and smells of land and sea.
As we look in awe and wonder
we are drawn into worshipping and praising you.

We look again and we see what we have turned this world into:
the brutality of war, humanity's inhumanity, the starving, the unloved.
With unanswered questions – 'How?', 'Why?'
we feel dry and distant from you.

Creator God, lead us into worship with you

Speaking God,

You speak to us through your scriptures,
through the words and music of others
through the gentle sounds of people going about their business
through sounds you have created: a babbling brook and roaring sea.
We listen appreciatively
and are drawn into worshipping and praising you.

Then we hear the sounds of our angry and threatening voices,
of bombs dropping, of innocent victims crying out in pain.
With unanswered questions – 'How?', 'Why?'
we feel dry and distant from you.

Speaking God, lead us into worship with you

Nourishing God,

You feed your children with many different flavours of food.
We are spoilt for choice.
You feed us through bread and wine,
we eat hungrily
and are drawn into worshipping and praising you.

Then we see others who have nothing,
have no idea when they will next eat,
babies who suckle at an empty breast,
with parents who can offer no more than arms to hold them
and hands to bury them.

We have no idea what it means to really pray, 'Give us this day our daily bread.'
We feel dry and distant from you.

Nourishing God, lead us into worship with you

Touching God,

You reach out to everyone, knowing us better than we know ourselves.
We thank you for the gift of touch,
the softness of a baby's skin, a pet's fur, warmth on a cold day,
and for the human touch, a handshake, caress and kiss.
As we receive your unconditional love
we are drawn into worshipping and praising you.

But many of your children still long to be loved,
craving the gentleness of human relationships,
but know nothing but loneliness or abuse, violence or neglect.
How easy it is to feel dry and distant from you.

Touching God, lead us into worship with you

Holy God, we know that however difficult it may be at times,
that worshipping you draws us in,
helps to mould us to the person that you want us to be,
helps us to bring your love into a broken world.
Help us to use all our senses in worshipping you.

Holy God, lead us into worship with you.

Amen

Prayers in preparation for a service

The following four prayers could perhaps be combined with a time of quiet, reflective
music and/or visuals as your service begins.

Dear Lord,

We gather here today in a quiet moment.
This is your time and your place.
Come close to us now as we prepare for worship.
We remember your goodness to us through our lives
and your love for us fresh every morning.
We thank you for the blessings received by us
as part of your worshipping church.
May we never take for granted all that you do for us.
Help us to praise you together in our worship today
and to recognise you in the ordinary things in our lives.

Bless those leading us in worship.
Bless all who have been part of preparing our service today.
May they feel your love and strength surrounding them.

Lord, bless us now as we go forward in your holy name.

Amen

Dear Lord,

In the quiet of the [evening/morning] we stand before you.
This is your time and your space.

You are here, Lord, waiting to listen and to speak.
Help us now in this time of worship to be still in ourselves
and to set aside all distractions and worries.

We ask for your blessing on the preparations for this service,
which have been made with love and care.

Bless those who are leading us in worship today.
May they feel your love and strength upholding them
as they preach your word.

Lord, bless us now as we go forward in your holy name.

Amen

Spirit of God,

We ask your blessing on those who are leading our worship today.
You have inspired them as they prepared for this service.
Continue to be with them now as they come to share your message with us.
May we all be open to the challenge and encouragement of the gospel.
For your kingdom's sake we pray.
Amen

God of all, we come before you today to bring you our worship.

We worship you in anticipation of the day when
'every knee shall bow to [God],
and every tongue shall give praise to God' (Romans 14:11).

We worship you remembering those who do not yet know you.

We worship you remembering those who are unable to gather in your name
because of fear of persecution.

We worship you remembering those who are unable to be here
due to ill-health, work or family commitments,
or reasons known only to you.

We worship you remembering those whose spiritual or mental ill-health
is such that they are unable to worship.

And so we bring you our words, our thoughts, our bodies and our lives
in the knowledge that if we worship 'in spirit and truth'
our worship will be pleasing and acceptable to you. (John 4).

Help us to worship you not only here and now,
but with our whole lives 'doing justice, loving kindness,
and walking humbly with our God' (Micah 6:8).

In the name of Jesus,

Amen

Different ways of praying

Creativity in worship

Are there creative skills in your congregation which are not currently used in **Worship**?

Could someone draw or paint a picture during **Worship** as a focus for the theme, in praise or as **Prayer**? Similarly, if you have someone with mime or graphic recording skills, they might 'illustrate' the scripture readings or sermon. This can be done using technology where installed, or on an easel or flipchart.

Collage is another technique which can involve one artist or many from the congregation. This might be the relatively simple collage of many faces cut from magazines (appropriate to praying for others; 'crowd' scenes such as feeding the 5,000; Old Testament passages such as the exodus; and for themes such as inclusivity, diversity, global concerns or community focus) or the creation of a rainbow to illustrate the flood.

There are many creative prayer suggestions in the Holy Habit booklet on **Prayer** which involve members of the congregation, in addition to more traditional suggestions such as drawing, making simple candle shapes or creating leaves for a prayer tree.

In a small congregation or café service, you might give each person a piece of modelling clay and ask them to form a shape (a person, star, stone, etc.) which can then be placed together as part of the prayers, as appropriate to the theme. In larger congregations, a few people might contribute.

In short, don't be afraid to use the gifts in the congregation sensitively and con-textually within **Worship**.

A gathering prayer

Light scented candles or lavender oil so that the smell has spread around the **Worship** space by the time people have gathered.

Sing 'May the fragrance of Jesus fill this place' as you gather for **Worship**.

N.B. Be aware that some people's breathing may be affected by strong smells.

A prayer of adoration

Ask the congregation to brainstorm attributes of God. Record them on a flipchart or screen.

Then pray a prayer of adoration.

As you name each attribute of God, encourage the congregation to applaud or to clap a simple rhythm that you have taught them.

Worship music

Invite people to share a time when a hymn or song has enabled them to **Worship** or to have a real sense of God's presence. Then sing the song or hymn together.

Find someone who listens to a Christian radio station or Christian worship music in their car and invite them to share their experience of worshipping in this way. Maybe share the music together. Invite others to try this way of **Worshipping**.

Using our bodies in worship

When it comes to **Worship**, the first commandment, to 'love the Lord your God with all your heart, and with all your soul, and with all your might' (Deuteronomy 6:5), is foundational. It emphasis the priority of **Worship** and also the wholeness of **Worship**. **Worship** is about offering all we are in response to God's giving to us.

In expressing **Worship**, there are many examples from the Bible and the Christian tradition (and indeed the Jewish tradition) of the whole of the body or parts of the body being used to express praise, adoration, humility and other offerings of devotion. We read of hands being lifted up or clapped together, people bowing or lying prostrate on the floor. Then there are those who dance and others who stand or sit in quiet contemplation. You might like to research these and think how some of these postures and gestures could be used in **Worship** – in services of worship but also as expressions of worship at home or out and about in the wonder of God's creation.

If you would like to encourage others to use their bodies more in **Worship**, think carefully how you go about this. People may need reassurance that this is okay biblically, and for some movement may be difficult or embarrassing or simply not possible.

Prayers for the persecuted

It is important to note that across the world, there are many people who can't meet together to **Worship** God, maybe because of persecution or because they are refugees. Maybe they are ill or living in fear.

Have a large map of the world pinned up or lying on the floor where people can easily access it. You may choose to have stories of persecuted or displaced Christians placed around the map (the Open Doors website might be helpful – **www. opendoorsuk.org**).

Encourage people to take a pin and to stick it into the map and pray for the Christians in that country who cannot meet together for whatever reason. You may like to encourage people to also pray for those in this country who are bullied or picked on for being a Christian, as well as those known to them who can't meet for **Worship** because of illness.

GROUP MATERIAL AND ACTIVITIES

Some of these small group materials are traditional Bible studies, some are more diverse session plans and others are short activities, reflections and discussions. Please choose materials appropriate to whatever group you are working with.

God-centred worship

Psalm 100; Ephesians 2:1–10; Romans 12:1–2

> All true worship is God-centred. As we acknowledge the mystery and glory of the eternal God, Father, Son and Holy Spirit, we are moved to offer our praise and confess our sins, confident of God's mercy and forgiveness. God's acts of grace and love in creation and salvation are recounted and celebrated, and we respond with thanksgiving, intercession and the offering of our lives.
>
> *The Methodist Worship Book* (1999), p. vii

This session looks at three passages of scripture which illustrate these themes. You may want to print copies of each passage for people to annotate or write thoughts on.

Psalm 100

Take time to read slowly through this short psalm. You may well be struck by the repeated encouragement to joy and delight in **Worship**. The source of such exuberance is not to be found simply in our emotions or circumstances, nor can it be artificially constructed. Rather, it comes when we recognise the truth about God.

Verse 3 celebrates God's very existence. The words 'Know that the Lord is God' invite our imaginations to run riot. All that we know of this energy-filled, expanding, beautiful, pulsating, mysterious, wonder-filled universe is, we believe, but a pointer to its creating source: the living God.

The last verse of the psalm spells out why joy, thanksgiving and praise are at the heart of **Worship**, for it speaks of God's character: God is good. Merciful love is the very heart of God's being, and God is truly faithful.

- What does it mean for you to delight in God? What helps you to do so?
- How do you delight in God when faced by tragedy, difficulty or grief?
- 'God is good. Merciful love is the very heart of God's being, and God is truly faithful.' How helpful are these words in expressing your experience of God?
- The psalm calls on all the earth to shout for joy. How does creation aid **Worship**?
- What is your experience of the **Worship** of people from other parts of the world? How has it enriched your own **Worship**?

Ephesians 2:1–10

The letter to the Ephesians is a little different to some of the other letters attributed to Paul. It may have been rather like a circular letter to a number of churches, and its language suggests that it could be used particularly in **Worship**. Its whole theme can be summed up as praise for God's act of salvation in Christ. In chapter 2, this saving work is spelled out in more detail.

Take time to read through the passage, underlining words that inspire you and circling words which you find challenging or invite questions.

Paul describes his readers as being 'dead'. This may well carry the sense that they were cut off from the life of God, which can only be experienced through a lively relationship in the risen Christ. Such a relationship and life, Paul stresses, cannot be achieved through human endeavour. It is God's gift. The reason for **Worship** and celebration is that God, by reason simply of love, has given us this gift.

So **Worship** is a celebration of life-giving grace. Paul speaks in verse 7 of the 'immeasurable riches of his grace'; in part, this richness is seen in the extent of grace – it is for everyone without distinction. In part, the richness is seen in the effectiveness of grace – it really works. Later in the letter (3:18, NIV), Paul prays that his readers will 'grasp how wide and long and high and deep is the love of Christ'.

- Read the words of Charles Wesley's hymn, 'What shall I do, my God to love' (below) and explore how far they reflect your own experience and thinking.
- Paul describes the human condition from which God rescues us in Christ as being 'dead through the trespasses and sins'. To what extent does that ring true for you? How would you describe the human condition?

What shall I do, my God to love,
My loving God to praise!
The length, and breadth, and height to prove
And depth of sovereign grace?

Thy sovereign grace to all extends,
Immense and unconfined;
From age to age it never ends,
It reaches all mankind.

Throughout the world its breadth is known,
Wide as infinity,
So wide it never passed by one;
Or it had passed by me.

My trespass was grown up to Heaven;
But far above the skies,
In Christ abundantly forgiven,
I see Thy mercies rise!

The depth of all-redeeming love,
What angel-tongue can tell?
O may I to the utmost prove
The gift unspeakable!

Come quickly, then, my Lord, and take
Possession of Thine own;
My longing heart vouchsafe to make
Thine everlasting throne.

Charles Wesley, *Hymns and Sacred Poems* (1742), some verses omitted

Romans 12:1–2

We've noted that **Worship**, properly understood, concentrates on God, Creator and Saviour. God's gracious mercy is thus a central theme. In the letter to Romans, the first eleven chapters contain a detailed and structured argument on how God's grace is accessed by faith and is thus available to all, without distinction. In chapter 12 and the following chapters, Paul spells out what it means for us to accept God's mercy for ourselves. The two verses which we have chosen set the whole scene. Read them through in as many translations as you can.

Note in verse 1 the language of sacrifice. Some of Paul's readers came from a pagan background, where their religious observance involved making the appropriate offerings and sacrifices at the temple of their chosen deity. Others among Paul's readers were Jewish, and so in part identified **Worship** with the sacrifices offered in the temple in Jerusalem. In each case, they would have understood that sacrifice involved offering something that was to be holy (i.e. set apart for God) and pleasing. Paul uses these words, but in so doing redefines the whole content of religion and **Worship**. We find a prelude to this thinking in parts of the Hebrew scriptures, where for instance Amos pleads for a religion of justice (Amos 5:21–24), and Micah urges a humble walk with God as more pleasing to God than animal sacrifices (Micah 6:8). Paul, however, takes it further when he states that spiritual **Worship** is all about offering our whole selves to God.

Verse 2 begins to explore how this works out. All around us there are words, ideas and actions which shape the way in which we approach life. To **Worship** means that we recognise this reality and constantly ask whether they are in harmony with the way of Christ. The transformation which renews and reshapes our thinking and our ability to discern God's will comes from within and is a long and deep process.

All this underlines that true, spiritual **Worship** is about more than what happens when we gather on a Sunday or in a house group. It involves being open to God's Spirit in our homes, in our work, in our leisure, so that we love what God would love and do what God would do.

- In what ways might **Worship** be part of, and affect, our daily decisions and activity?
- Paul's words apply to the church as well as to individuals. What steps can we take to allow a shared transformed mind to guide and energise our church life?

Engaging in worship ᛉᚾᛉ

Psalm 117

Read Psalm 117, a song telling everyone in the world to **Worship** God.

Ask the group to think about all the different ways you can **Worship** God – encourage them to think about the different senses and parts of the body. Some suggestions follow in case you need to prompt their thinking:

- with your voice (by singing, by finding out how to praise God in different languages)
- with your eyes (by looking at and enjoying God's beautiful world)
- with your ears (by listening to a Bible story, by listening to others)
- with your feet (by dancing your 'thank you' to God during a **Worship** song)
- with your mind (by reflecting on a Bible story in silence)
- with your hands (by clapping your hands, by making something colourful to show God your thoughts or to give to someone as a gift, by showing 'kind hands' in the way you treat other people, by doing ordinary things – like tidying up – with 'great love')
- with your actions (by being 'the best that you can be', by trying to live the Holy Habits).

Ask what people's favourite way to **Worship** God is. Challenge them to choose a different way to try **Worshipping** God.

Finish with a prayer:

> Dear God,
>
> Thank you that there are so many different ways to worship you.
> However we are feeling, whatever we are doing,
> help us never to forget to worship you and to thank you for your love.
>
> Amen

Now that's what I call worship! 👪

This activity is an opportunity to ask people what they think about the **Worship** that they have experienced and to reflect upon what is important in **Worship**. Although this session may be more suited to young people, it would be a great opportunity to hear the views of different age groups in a congregation.

Set the scene the week before and explain to the group that they are going to be 'mystery worshippers'. That means that they will attend a **Worship** service, but they will be reflecting upon it and answering questions about it. Their thoughts will be shared in the next group session. You could ask the people to go to their usual service or encourage them to go to a different church's service that they don't normally attend.

Ask them to consider the questions which follow. It may be helpful to give them these on a form on which they fill in their answers.

- Did you feel welcomed in the service?
- List the different parts of the service.
- In which parts of the service did you feel most connected with God?
- Were there any parts of the service which distracted you from God?
- Do you think how you were feeling on the day affected your experience in the service?
- Did the number of people present make any difference to your experience of **Worship**?
- What were your overall impressions of the **Worship** service?
- If you had to pick one part of the service where you felt that you were truly **Worshipping** God, what would it be?

Discuss these questions as a group using any further follow-up questions that you think necessary. Sometimes people, often young people in particular, may have strong opinions about **Worship** and would like to change it. Help them to think through practical ways in which they may help bring about change in **Worship** in their church, if it is something they feel strongly about.

Now, present the group with the following scenario.

Due to a devastating war, a new community has been established on a previously uninhabited island. The community has lived together for quite a while and you have discovered about 40 people of different ages who are Christians. You decide that it would be a good idea to gather the 40 people to spend some time **Worshipping** God together. There is one communal building on the island which is a large rectangular room. You are starting from scratch and can create a time to **Worship** God together in any way that you would like. What would you create?

- What would you include?
- What should the room look like?
- How should the time together be led (or not)?
- How long should you meet for?
- What should be the most important thing about the **Worship**?
- What would you bring to the **Worship**?
- What sort of experience would you want people to have?

You could allow the group to work in pairs or threes on their plans and then share their ideas with the rest of the group. Hopefully you should be able to draw out what they think is important in an act of **Worship**.

Help them to think through that **Worship** is about what they are offering to God, and to reflect upon which traditions in **Worship** they chose to continue on the island and why that was important.

Finish the exercise with some 'I wonder' questions about the scenario:

- I wonder what it felt like for the people on the island to **Worship** alone?
- I wonder why it was important for them to come together?
- I wonder what it felt like to **Worship** with other people after a long time without the opportunity?
- I wonder what God thinks about our **Worship** service?

Allow the group to reflect on these questions and offer some answers. Encourage them to think of their own 'I wonder' questions on the topic of **Worship**.

Wonder and amazement

Psalm 8, Luke 2:25–38

It will be helpful to have the following resources to hand: Bibles or copies of the passages; star-shaped notes or cards; a large sheet of blue paper; pictures of tiny babies, including a tiny hand or foot; a copy of the Methodist booklet *Holiness and Justice* or access to the internet to see Ric Stott's picture (see p. 35); words or recording of 'Everyday God' by Bernadette Farrell.

After welcoming the group, encourage them to sit comfortably, to close their eyes and, as they listen to the opening words of scripture, ask them to try to visualise the scene, paying attention to the images that come to mind.

Psalm 8
- Invite the group to describe the images in their minds. Particularly notice the adjectives. Are there words about scale?
- How do you feel as you listen to this passage?

There can be few people who haven't gazed up into the night sky at some time in their life, and wondered at the infinite dazzle of the stars. Yet the psalmist sees beyond the stars to the God who made them; his words praise Creator, not just creation.

Stargazing is a rare treat for those who live in cities. The sky, though ablaze with stars, is dimmed by smog and light pollution. And so we live apart from the stars' constant reminder of the infinite universe, which was as familiar as sunshine to the author of this psalm. Though we know more of the depths of space, we see less.

- Take a moment to pause and think about the enormity of the universe and the God who created and fills it. Choose one word to reflect back to God and write this on a star-shaped card (or draw a star on a small piece of paper). Invite people to place their stars on a large sheet of paper in the centre of the group. Read again verses 1, 3, 4 and 9 from Psalm 8 as a prayer of adoration to God.

We are not all stargazers. Our second reading invites us to witness wonder on a very different scale. Again, invite the group to sit comfortably and picture the scene as the passage is read.

Luke 2:25–38
- Did anything stand out as you pictured the scene in the temple?
- Have you ever held a very young child in your arms? If so, what did you notice?
- Divide the group into two halves. Ask one group to think about how Simeon might have felt on that day, and the other to consider Anna's feelings. Ask each group to feed back to the other in the form 'When I held/saw that baby I felt…'
- How does a sense of wonder contribute to the story?
- How do we feel when we unexpectedly encounter Jesus?
- What links can the group draw between this passage and Psalm 8?

For Simeon and Anna, this special baby brought more wonder and joy than any other, as they shared with Mary and Joseph the knowledge that this baby was God's Messiah, the light for the Gentiles, and were filled with praise for God.

We need to hear the invitation at the heart of these texts, the invitation to wonder and amazement. For there is so much to wonder at: the dazzle of the stars, the forces that hold atoms in balance, the intricacies of physical being. All this is God's work, and both texts recognise it as such, and begin and end with praise of God.

But the texts also challenge us to recognise the responsibility which God entrusts to us. Holding a tiny baby is an act of immense responsibility. And the psalm too reminds us that our wonder at God's creation is coupled with responsibility for it. Why has God given us dominion (as in Genesis 1:28), especially when we seem to be so spectacularly bad at caring for God's creation?

Perhaps the answer lies precisely in our capacity for wonder and amazement – if we let it flourish within us. Astronaut Tim Peake delighted the world with his images from space – sunset over the edge of the whole planet. But so often we take it all for granted and don't see the glory – and then we fail in our God-given task of stewarding this wonderful world; it becomes mundane, tedious, boring, and so we become careless and inattentive.

So, can we deliberately try to cultivate and develop our capacity for wonder? Artist and Methodist minister Ric Stott reflected on this in his picture 'The beyond brought close, the mundane made strange', available in the Methodist *Holiness and Justice* booklet or on his blog at **www.iaskforwonder.com** (search his blog for 'Holiness & Justice 2'). He invites us to recognise that everyday life can bring us the unexpected, breathtaking moment just as much as the depths of space, as we see something familiar in a new light, in a strange context. The poet Gerard Manley Hopkins wrote of how 'the world is charged with the grandeur of God', and how 'there lives the dearest freshness, deep down things'. When we learn to recognise the glory of God revealed in the ordinary and everyday, then we shall fulfil the responsibilities of stewardship which God has laid in our hands.

- Invite the group to comment on Stott's picture or the words from Hopkins' poem.
- What inspires you with a sense of awe? How has this developed over time?
- What relationship is there between our **Worship** (privately or in church) and a sense of wonder? How can we build this up?

Prayer
- Spend a few moments remembering the last time you were filled with wonder, and thank God for that. If the group wishes, you could also share your stories with each other.
- What responsibilities for stewarding God's creation do you hold? Pray for one another in these responsibilities, and for all who share in the task of stewarding.
- Sing or listen to 'Everyday God' by Bernadette Farrell (StF 45).
- Finish with a closing prayer:

God of the distant stars and the newborn child,
Help us to open our eyes and see your glory
Help us to live as people filled with wonder and amazement
So that we can pay full attention to the needs of your wonderful world
Amen

Follow-on activities
- Go outside on a clear night and see how many stars you can spot.
- Try making a 'wonderbook' – like a scrap book, but recording pictures or words that make you think 'Wow!', alerting you to God's presence. Wonderful to go back to in years to come.

FORMING THE HABIT

The ideas presented in this section are offered to help you establish or further practise **Worship** as a regular habit personally, as a church and in engagement with your local community and the wider world. You may want to consider using the ideas in more than one of these contexts.

In developing **Worship** as a regular habit, you may find some of the material in the 'Understanding the habit' section helpful too.

STORIES TO SHOW THE HABIT FORMING

How could you use these formative and transformative stories to inspire others? What stories of your own could you share?

Can work be worshipful? Can our daily labour give glory to God? These were questions that lay at the heart of the creation of the Green Cross Co-op, a Christian workers' cooperative in Gloucester. Methodist Minister Simon Topping takes up the story:

> Those involved in setting up the Green Cross Co-op were convinced that many forms of work and employment were far from worshipful. We knew of people struggling to get by on poverty wages, or living with job insecurity, or participating in economic activity that was damaging to people and planet. We could also sense a spirit of alienation in many workplaces that didn't glorify God: alienation between worker and owner, between worker and the product of their work, even alienation between worker and worker.

> We believed that, for Christians, the workers' co-operative model would help to tackle this sense of alienation and provide a significant step towards bringing work and **Worship** together. In a workers' co-operative, the enterprise is owned by all the members and decisions are made democratically and, ideally, with a consensus – a bit like a church! We felt it embodied the *koinonia* or **Fellowship** which is so important to a worshipping community.

> We also felt that, to be worshipful, we needed to work in harmony with God's creation, rather than against it. Our delivery service was pedal-powered, by bicycle and cargo-trike, we ran a refill service for eco-friendly cleaning products and collected recyclables from two charities.

> Finally, we sought to draw on the resources of the monastic tradition who interwove their daily labour with their daily office. So, we wrote and used a set of working-day prayers in which we prayed that, 'in Christ, our work may be transformed into a labour of love, an act of **Worship**, a manifestation of your kingdom'.

In his book *Holy Habits* (Malcolm Down Publishing, 2016), Andrew Roberts invites people to 'imagine the whole of life being offered in **Worship**. God being glorified in the harvesting of the crop, the styling of the hair, the satellite being launched'. One disciple of Jesus who seeks to do just that is Andy Haynes.

When Andy worked as a car salesman, he tuned the radios of all the new cars he sold to the station 'Premier Praise' as an act of **Worship** and as a means of introducing his customers to contemporary **Worship**.

In his present role as 'Hands-On' Estate Manager at a country hall, much of Andy's work is outside where he loves sharing life with nature – being part of the weather, the drama of the storm and the joy of the sunshine. There he says, 'I hear the bird songs and feel the breeze, and because of all this I find myself humming hymns such as "Morning has broken" and, the favourite of many, "How great thou art!" It makes me conscious of our creator God as I go about my duties and I am able to **Worship** as I work.'

Every day, many Christian teachers introduce children to Jesus, the Bible and prayer. One such teacher is Shona, who says:

For many children, their first experience of Christian **Worship** is in school. It is wonderful to see the sense of awe in them as they encounter God in **Worship**, in creation and in particular the fabulous and often funny stories that Jesus told.

How might you pray for and support the Christian teachers in your church? And how might you offer acts of **Worship** in your local schools or hospitality to schools who would love to visit your church?

Alex had been attending Messy Church with his mum for two years when he told her he wanted to be baptised. A leader there takes up the story:

Through the fun, friendship, craft, games, singing, prayer, Bible stories and food – all of which is part of our **Worship** together, he had come to know Jesus to be his friend and saviour. At eight years old, he was able to affirm his faith and make the baptismal promises for himself and rejoice that his little sister was also baptised on the same day. He said on his baptism day, 'God, I want to be christened because I want to be in your lovely family. I love Messy Church and I hope that April and me have a wonderful time.'

PRACTICES TO HELP FORM THE HABIT

Here are some suggestions for how **Worship** can be part of a rhythm or rule of life in our personal discipleship and in and through the **Fellowship** of our churches.

When the Fresh Expressions agency produced its first DVD, there were a number of stories that grabbed people's attention. One was Messy Church, which has gone on to bloom in thousands of places. Another was Legacy XS in Benfleet, Essex (now known as Legacy Youth Congregation). Based in a skateboard park, the sight of younger people **Worshipping** God on boards and BMX bikes was eye-opening and thought-provoking for many people – of all ages. It spoke powerfully of the value of creating opportunities for **Worship** that allowed people to offer gifts from their culture as expressions of praise.

While the style of **Worship** at Legacy (**www.facebook.com/LegacyXS**) may be radically different, the underlying principles and values are thoroughly orthodox. Via its website, the church explains:

> At the heart of our community is the cross of Jesus. We worship him together as Lord and Saviour, filled with his Holy Spirit and led to the throne of our Father as returning prodigals – forgiven and deeply loved. We recognise our weakness and worship him, Father, Son and Spirit, as best we can with all the resources he pours out upon us to make this possible.

For Legacy, **Worship** is not just an activity but a way of life. They see themselves as a community living their journey as an act of **Worship**:

> An outward-looking people concerned with the needs of their wider community and working for justice.

Legacy Youth Congregation lives out the concluding words of the definition of a fresh expression of church, as offered by the Fresh Expressions agency, as it is 'shaped by the gospel and the enduring marks of the church and for its cultural context'. In your context, might you develop a fresh expression of church to share the gospel and enable others to **Worship** God, using the gifts of their culture?

Often (daily or weekly)

> ## Journalling
>
> Journalling is regularly reflecting on your experiences, thoughts and encounters with God and keeping a note of your reflections. See the Holy Habits Introductory Guide for more information.
>
> As you try to develop the habit of **Worship**, write about the worship you have experienced. Reflect upon when you found worshipping God easy and when a challenge. When did you feel you were truly worshipping God? Note the factors that helped you worship – were they external or internal? When you look back at your journal, do you notice any changes in the way that you worship or your approach to it? When have you noticed **Worship** becoming a habit that impacts your discipleship?

Worship in the everyday

Each day, pray that what you do and who you are will be offerings of **Worship**.

On a daily basis, take time to stop for a moment or two and notice the glory of God around you in nature, in the smile of the elderly person or the chuckle of a baby, in the miracle of electricity or the healing skills of the doctors and nurses. Make a practice of turning pauses into praise.

Before you retire for the night, bring to mind three ways in which you have been blessed and let it lead you into **Worship**, offering praise and thanks.

Individually, as family, with friends or as a church, develop a simple pattern of daily **Worship**. There are lots of resources that can help you with this, or you can develop your own with a psalm or a song, a prayer and a simple symbolic act. How do you build habits of **Worship** into your time working, at school or in your own home?

On the way to work, listen to some Christian **Worship** on your phone or in the car. Let that **Worship** shape your day. If you spend most of your time at home, why not make a practice of sharing in a daily act of **Worship** on the radio via Radio 4, UCB or Premier Radio (all available on digital radio as well as via the internet).

Whole-life worship

As noted in the introduction to this habit, **Worship** is a whole-life activity. It is a way of life. As you consciously take time to explore this habit, imagine the whole of your life, personally and collectively, being offered in **Worship**. God being glorified in your daily life and work, your relationships with others, your welcoming of the stranger, your campaigning for justice.

Let Colossians 3:17 be your companion as you explore this habit:

> Whatever you do, in word or deed, do everything in the name of the Lord Jesus, giving thanks to God the Father through him.

When you gather for **Worship**, strive for opportunities to offer in praise, lament and prayer the joys and hurts of the world to the heart of God, and seek to craft **Worship** that inspires the worshippers to go out and touch that world with holy, healing hands to the glory of God.

Sometimes (weekly or monthly)

Worship in a different way

It is good to **Worship** in regular patterns and places. But worshipping in different ways can help to keep your worshipping life fresh. Why not explore different ways of **Worshipping**, using art, music, icons, movement or other practices which you are less familiar with. What do you find helpful about these practices? How can they inform your regular practices of **Worship**? What could you adopt into your habits of **Worship**?

Individually, or as a small group or youth group, plan an act of **Worship** for a different group in your church.

Consider offering (or supporting those already offering) services of **Worship** in residential homes, schools, hospitals, or with the housebound. There are many chaplaincy resources available to help with this, explored in other Holy Habits.

Intentionally craft acts of **Worship** that are particularly suitable to those who are not regular worshippers – **Worship** can be a part of **Making More Disciples**. How might those on the fringe of regular worship contribute to designing such opportunities? For example, using their gifts, contributing spaces and sharing testimonies.

Meetings

Meetings are part of being church – so how are your meetings an act of **Worship**? How could they be offered to God and conducted in a spirit of **Worship**, beyond a quick prayer at the beginning and/or end of the meeting?

Occasionally (quarterly, annually)

Worship in different places

Join with other Christians of different denominations or traditions to **Worship** with them. Notice what you enjoy. Might this be something you could encourage your local church to offer? And notice what you miss from your own tradition. Might this be something you could offer to others?

With appropriate permissions, **Worship** in a public space. Let that **Worship** be both a witness and an offering on behalf of that community. Celebrate God's greatness in the midst of creation. Early morning on Easter day or Pentecost are both great times for this. Why not have an outdoor Harvest Festival at the local market or farm?

Go to a Christian festival and allow yourself to get lost 'in the wonder, love and praise' of the **Worship** offered.

Consider developing a different regular act of **Worship** or a fresh expression of church for those who struggle with your church's preferred style of **Worship**.

Many churches plan 'pulpit exchanges' to help congregations engage with different ministers, often of different denominations. Why not consider that or, instead of the preachers moving, could the congregations swap churches for one Sunday? This might be particularly appropriate to do as an activity for a Churches Together group during the week of prayer for Christian Unity, for example.

If you are feeling radical, join with congregations who have 'given up church' for Lent (for example, see **www.getoutofchurchsunday.co.uk**), using the time they would normally spend in services to engage in their communities.

Refresh your understanding of worship

Even if you are not a designated or authorised leader of **Worship**, why not participate in a course for worship leaders to understand and appreciate more of the theology and practices of collective worship.

Whole-life worship

Nine out of ten people will be outside of church walls on Mondays, Tuesdays, etc… yet a key question is often overlooked: how do we aid people to be church on Monday to Saturday, so that every day is special and not just Sunday?

Those who come into our Sunday sanctuaries come from real communities where they are often 'between a rock and hard place'. We may be unaware of their experiences, for example living in a place of genteel poverty, real biting deprivation and threat of redundancy, domestic violence, knife crime, bullying at school, intimidation in the work place or mental ill-health. Further, many experience the cruel bite of physical loneliness or crushing spiritual loneliness. The gospel banquet of Sunday needs a slow release quality and signposts for seven days.

There is a great range of resources available to help with thinking and activity around 24/7, whole-life **Worship**. Alongside resources offered by your church, 24/7 Prayer, the London Institute for Contemporary Christianity, Scripture Union and Fresh Expressions have lots of stories to inspire and resources to help. There are also helpful resources that can be gifted to others to help them discover the wonder of **Worship**.

Increasingly, more churches are open at lunchtime or all day, and it can be rewarding to join an ecumenical group sharing Holy Communion and then return to work. Workplace chaplains are a rich resource and are available in a host of contexts and Prayer/Quiet Rooms are developing in factories, universities, retail centres and even casinos! They are open to all, and can offer lovely encounters with others of different faith positions, enabling discreet yet life-giving conversations to manifest so that we realise we are not alone on the Emmaus Road. The joy of sharing faith stories with a Muslim or Hindu colleague can be illuminating upon one's own faith and pattern of sustaining midweek devotion.

To explore further, consider inviting local chaplains to highlight how they offer faith encounters and engagement at work.

Review your welcome

Before we go into a place we make decisions, even unconsciously, about whether we want to go in and what we think it will be like inside. If we decide to go in, we quickly decide if it's 'our kind of place' or not. If our churches want to attract children and young people, we need to put some thought in before they are even there, so that they will want to come in and, if they do come through our doors, they will quickly feel, 'ah, this is my kind of place', and 'I am welcome here'.

Here's a task for churches: stand outside your church building, imagine you are (a) a parent with toddlers, (b) a 4-year-old, (c) a 13-year-old, (d) a single adult, (e) a wheelchair user, (f) an elderly person and ask yourself these questions:

1. As I stand outside: is this a place that is for me? (How would you know?)
2. As I walk in: is this 'my kind of place'? What is there to show that this place is ready for me to be here?
3. Where would I be comfortable here?
4. How will people respond if they notice me?
5. As I walk in, do I feel 'Phew, wonderful' or 'Uh oh, I'd best get out of here'?
6. What will I be able to see or do during the service? Is there something interesting for me?

Review your worship

Young people and children now grow up in an education system which attempts at all times to engage and involve them. We can learn from this if we want to engage with young people and children in **Worship**, and it may even make it more joyful for all of us! Some questions for your church:

- Is it obvious that children and young people are wanted in this church? How?
- How welcome do children and young people feel in the Sunday service?
- How are our young people and children involved in the worshipping life and decision-making of the church?
- What is there about **Worship** here that would make a child or young person want to come back? Is there anything off-putting?

We sometimes speak of children and young people as the future, but they are the present, too, and can be part of things now! Jesus was very clear that children are welcome with God. How can we make sure that message comes across loud and clear?

QUESTIONS TO CONSIDER AS A CHURCH

These questions will help your church to consider how it can review the place of **Worship** in all of its life together. They are intended to be asked regularly rather than considered once and then forgotten. You will need to determine where in your church the responsibility for each question lies – with the whole church in a general meeting, or with the church leadership, a relevant committee or another grouping. Feel free to add more of your own.

- Reflect upon the whole life of the local church that you are part of. In what ways does **Worship** pervade its whole life? When, where and how is **Worship** expressed and experienced?
- If worship is about the things that we think are of worth, or of value, what does **Worship** at your church reveal about the things that you value?
- Are there times/places when a sense of whole-life **Worship** is missing?
- If **Worship** involves 'focusing on and celebrating God's presence', are there things in your church premises or services that help or hinder this?
- The Bible warns against the worship of idols. Are there things in your church that may have become idols – they are not of central importance but are treated as essential ingredients of collective worship?
- How much of your church budget is allocated to resourcing **Worship**? How does this compare to other areas?
- If God is always looking to make all things new (Revelation 21:5), how does this apply to the **Worship** you offer as a church?
- How do you encourage young children and families to feel part of your **Worship**? Can you make your worship area more welcoming for young children?
- What might need to be done to make collective **Worship** more accessible for people of different ethnicities, cultures, ages and physical abilities?
- Aside from the practicalities of choosing hymns, giving out hymn books etc., how could different people prepare for services of **Worship**?
- How do we ensure that those who prepare and lead acts of **Worship** are 'fed' themselves?
- How can you help people to continue their **Worship** seven days a week?
- How are the needs and joys of the local community and the wider world offered in **Worship**?
- As we strive for excellence in our **Worship**, how do we judge its quality? Are some people inhibited from fully participating in **Worship** because they feel under-qualified or inadequate?

CONNECTING THE HABITS

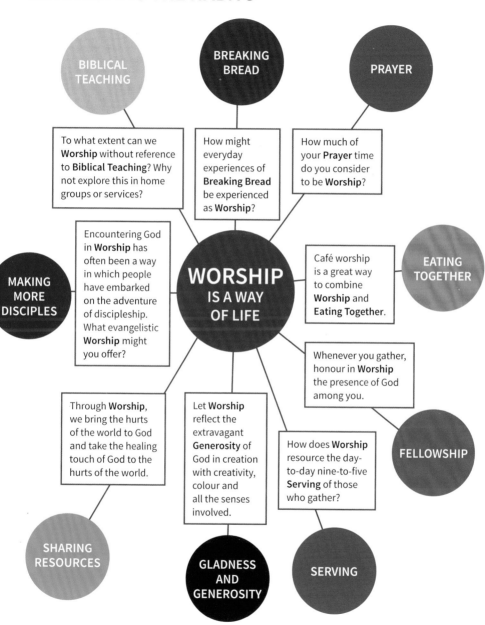

BIBLICAL TEACHING

BREAKING BREAD

PRAYER

To what extent can we **Worship** without reference to **Biblical Teaching**? Why not explore this in home groups or services?

How might everyday experiences of **Breaking Bread** be experienced as **Worship**?

How much of your **Prayer** time do you consider to be **Worship**?

Encountering God in **Worship** has often been a way in which people have embarked on the adventure of discipleship. What evangelistic **Worship** might you offer?

MAKING MORE DISCIPLES

WORSHIP
IS A WAY OF LIFE

EATING TOGETHER

Café worship is a great way to combine **Worship** and **Eating Together**.

Whenever you gather, honour in **Worship** the presence of God among you.

Through **Worship**, we bring the hurts of the world to God and take the healing touch of God to the hurts of the world.

Let **Worship** reflect the extravagant **Generosity** of God in creation with creativity, colour and all the senses involved.

How does **Worship** resource the day-to-day nine-to-five **Serving** of those who gather?

FELLOWSHIP

SHARING RESOURCES

GLADNESS AND GENEROSITY

SERVING

GOING FURTHER WITH THE HABIT

DEVELOPING FURTHER PRACTICES OF WORSHIP

Inclusive language in worship: a charter

We will encourage all those participating in **Worship** to use language which is inclusive; seeking to eliminate language which is exclusive on the grounds of human divisions such as age, class, disability, ethnicity, gender, race, or sexuality.

By doing this, we will help widen and expand our understanding of one another before God; helping us to develop our understanding of what it means to say that we are equal, made in the image of God (Genesis 1:27); that in Christ 'there is no longer Jew or Greek… slave or free… male and female' (Galatians 3:28).

We will do this by:

- Using translations of the Bible 'which avoid generic masculine terminology' (V. Faull & J. Sinclaire, *Count Us In: Inclusive language in liturgy*, Grove Books, 1986, p. 26).
- Choosing litanies and liturgy with inclusive language.
- Choosing hymns and **Worship** songs that are inclusive, altering words where legal and appropriate.
- Providing training for all those involved in the planning and leading of **Worship**.
- Informing the congregation, church members and adherents of these guidelines and seeking to help them understand the issues involved.

We will review our guidelines annually.

We also commit to exploring further both expansive language and the non-verbal language we use which might give subconscious signals of exclusivity.

Worshipping with those who have dementia

People with dementia are all different. There is no set pattern for enabling **Worship**. Elements that are familiar to those of a worshipping tradition will be helpful. However, do give attention to enabling an awareness of God's presence in their present lives, whether this is just for the moment or to be held for longer.

Some tips

- Plan the **Worship** but be flexible if the congregation deviates from your plan.
- Keep the service short (15–25 minutes).
- There is place for both formal and informal types of **Worship**. Visual and tactile aids can be useful.
- As far as is possible, involve people in the **Worship**.
- Use familiar hymns. Avoid a multiplicity of photocopied sheets.
- Choose familiar readings and prayers and use an appropriate version of the Bible.
- No sermon, but perhaps a 'thought for the day'.
- Use of symbols to give clues and cues as to what is happening.
- Try to include a personal blessing.
- Praying with eyes shut can make people feel disconnected, so keep them open!

Holy Communion

A service of Holy Communion can be important for those living with dementia. Knowing the people will help you judge how much liturgy is helpful. It could be that saying the words of institution, together with extempore prayers, is sufficient. Offering the elements together (intinction) can help reduce confusion. If possible, ask by name if they would like to receive the elements. If they say no, then offer a blessing.

Reflect upon what works and what is good, and be prepared to modify the style of the service in the light of your experience.

Enabling prayer in dementia

Praying with those who are living with dementia is not, or should not, be very different from praying with anyone else, but their situation does encourage us to be more creative and less cerebral, to be aware of senses and emotions rather than creating thoughts and words, to create a moment rather than rely on recollection as a basis for prayer.

For those with a background of Christian worship, familiar prayers may be helpful, although for those with advanced dementia meaning will fade while the words may remain with them.

For those without a faith background, prayer will be a whole new adventure with God, which we must be careful not to restrict by our own experience.

Joanna Collicutt's book *Thinking of You* (BRF, 2017) is a very helpful resource, and contains other service outlines and ideas for churches.

The Generations Project in Solihull offers some examples of active **Worship** and prayer in different seasons in the year (**www.generationssolihull.org.uk/marking-times--seasons.html**).

A 'moment' for prayer is created through some appropriate activity. Prayer can then capture the feelings and senses, either shared in a group or naturally as part of a conversation with a helper.

Worship and presence

Often the first thing that comes to mind when we hear the word **Worship** is a service that we go to. For many people, the 'going to' is not possible. Thankfully there are alternatives.

There are opportunities to **Worship** via the media, through scheduled radio, television and internet acts of worship. Many major Christian conferences and festivals now broadcast their **Worship** via the internet. If you know of people who are housebound, why not share with them, as an expression of **Fellowship**, a service of worship via the radio, television or internet in their home.

Technology is opening up opportunities to engage in **Worship** in a myriad of ways. Online church such as i-church (**www.i-church.org**) provide opportunities to **Worship** on your own or with others. Websites such as the Methodist Church website (**www.methodist.org.uk**) have resources for daily **Prayer** and **Worship**. Daily patterns of **Worship** can be resourced by online resources that can be accessed by download or smart phone. A worship CD in the car can encourage blessing rather than cursing whilst crawling to work through the traffic jams.

God is present and can be worshipped anywhere and everywhere. How might you use the resources available to make **Worship** more of a habit and to support those for whom accessing collective worship would otherwise be very difficult or impossible?

Sharing your story

During a **Worship** service invite people to share their stories of **Worshipping** in different settings – people may have been to a different church or a Christian festival. Some people may have stories to share of how they **Worship** God as they walk the dog, or dig the compost, or clean the house.

To follow on, those people could further share their story in an experiential way by taking someone else with them to **Worship** in their different place or way.

Plan a time when people can share those experiences, reporting back on the joys or challenges they have encountered.

ARTS AND MEDIA

There are many films and books containing scenes about **Worship** which could be used as an illustration in **Worship**. However, it is suggested that the following films and books are watched or read in their entirety and followed by a discussion to go deeper into the topic of **Worship**.

Films

👪 Billionaire Boy (U, 2016, 1h)

Society pursues wealth and status but money can't buy everything, as Len and his son find out when he develops a new kind of toilet roll.

- Does this film challenge you to reassess your priorities and relationships?
- Prayerfully consider how far you worship wealth, status or possessions.

You might also consider *Gangsta Granny* (U, 2013, 1h) – the story of a young boy whose parents want him to become a 'celebrity dancer' when all he wants is to become a plumber, or *Mr Stink* (U, 2012, 1h) – the story of a smelly old tramp with more to him than meets the eye. They can be used to explore issues of **Worship** in relation to celebrity culture and current affairs/news respectively.

All three are adapted from books by David Walliams.

Leap of Faith (PG, 1992, 1h48m)

Promoted as a romantic comedy, this film raises some important questions about **Worship**, emotion and signs and wonders. It exposes the risks, dangers and hypocrisies of hype and fraudulent behaviour in **Worship**, but also promotes the values of sincere faith and real relationships.

- How do we avoid manipulation in **Worship**, whilst allowing God to be God?

Rev (15, 2011 onwards, 30m episodes) – especially series 1 episode 2

Revd Adam Smallbone and his congregation raise questions familiar to many **Worshipping** communities:

- 'Where 2 or 3 are gathered in my name…' – does size matter when it comes to a **Worshipping** congregation?
- Does God only listen to those who shout the loudest – are loud music and quiet reflection equally valid forms of **Worship**?

- How do 'acts of **Worship**' relate to the day-to-day reality of our lives?

Silence (15, 2016, 2h41m / 15, 1971, 2h9m)

Two Jesuit priests travel to Japan to spread Catholicism and to locate their mentor.

- How can we **Worship** God when God seems absent or silent?

Sister Act (PG, 1992, 1h40m)

When a nightclub singer who has witnessed a horrific gang crime is disguised by the police as a nun in a traditional convent, neither the convent nor the singer will ever be the same.

- What does this film have to teach us about stepping outside our 'comfort zones'?
- What might we learn about the exuberance and sincerity of **Worship**?

Books: fiction

Are there people in your church or local community who would like to discuss some of these books at a book club? Guidance on how to form these is widely available online, and you could also ask denominational training officers for help.

👪 A Friend for Little Bear
Harry Horse (Walker Books, 1996)

Little Bear gets so distracted by all the things that keep washing up on his small island that he forgets his best friend, Horse. It isn't until Horse is washed away in the tide that Little Bear realises that Horse is the most special thing of all in his life. There is a happy ending when Horse is found again.

As Christians, we may want to say that Horse represents Jesus/God and that a friendship with Jesus is the thing that is of most worth in our lives.

Glory
Marilyn Kok (Multnomah, 1995)

Visiting Taiwan held adventure and love for beautiful widow Mariel Forrest, and also revealed a transforming encounter with God. This will challenge you to think deeply about who God is, how we encounter him and the ways he reveals himself to us.

👪 Good Good Father
Chris Tomlin (Thomas Nelson, 2016)

A little bear goes to visit the king to ask for help when the townspeople are in trouble. He has many adventures along the way as he tries to work out how to please the king, but ends up discovering just how much the king loves them and wants to help them. This will help primary school-aged children understand about God's unconditional love.

Reunion
Karen Ball (Multnomah, 1996)

A wonderful story about two people who learn to trust and to love again through their shared interest in nature. As they open themselves up to one another, they also open themselves up to God's love for them and grow closer to God and each other through shared experience. Scripture readings are interspersed into the story.

Books: non-fiction

Breakfast with God
(Quiet Moments with God)
Honor Books (2005)

This book is full of inspirational stories to read as you enjoy sharing breakfast with God each day. There is a scripture reference and reflective story for each new day. There are also companion books in this series for you to share a Coffee Break, Teatime and Sunset with God.

Facedown
Matt Redman (Kingsway Publications, 2004)

Matt Redman says, 'When we face up to the glory of God, we find ourselves face down in worship.' This is a challenging read about how we should be **Worshipping** God.

☺ **Here I Am to Worship**
Tim Hughes (Survivor Kingsway, 2009)

This book is recommended for teens. It describes **Worship** as a time of **Fellowship** with God; and discusses planning and preparation for **Worship**, especially focusing on the use of music.

Pray, Love, Remember
Michael Mayne (Darton, Longman & Todd, 1998)

A book describing the author's time as Dean of Westminster Abbey.

The Weaver, the Word and Wisdom: Worshipping the triune God
Michaela Youngson (Inspire, 2007)

An inspirational book packed full of ideas which can be used for personal reflection or small groups. The book encourages the reader to explore their understanding of the Trinity and personal relationship with God and is also an excellent resource for those leading **Worship** as it offers reflections, prayers, poems and creative ideas.

The Worship-Driven Life: The reason we were created
A.W. Tozer (Monarch Books, 2008)

The supreme importance of **Worship**: the purpose of humankind and the expectation of God.

Articles and online media

Good News Stories

Create Talk exhibition at Sutton Coldfield United Reformed church (**youtu.be/bzexOKLVU_Y** or search YouTube for 'Good News Stories with Nick').

Music

The following musical items may help you to explore and reflect further on this habit.

Hallelujah
Leonard Cohen

Messiah
G.F. Handel

Praise You in this Storm
Casting Crowns

The Heart of Worship
Matt Redman

Poetry

A number of poems are referenced below. Choose one to reflect on.

You may wish to consider some of the following questions:

- What does this poem say to you about **Worship**?
- Which images do you find helpful or unhelpful?
- How is your practice of **Worship** challenged by this poem?
- Could you write a poem to share with others the virtues of **Worship**?

Spoken Worship: Living words for personal and public prayer
Gerard Kelly (Zondervan, 2007)

A book of poems to be read aloud or silently, suitable for use in **Worship**, shared with groups or read privately. There are poems for different settings and occasions, as well as performance notes to enhance the power and contribution of poetry in **Worship**.

Devotions 1 – You: My Beginning
Ian Adams, from *Unfurling* (Canterbury Press, 2015)

Sabbath Song
Carla A. Grosch-Miller, from *Psalms Redux* (Canterbury Press, 2014)

A New Song
Michael Symmons Roberts, from *Drysalter* (Jonathan Cape, 2013)

Three Kings

David Jones (1895–1974): engraved woodblock, 1925, 10 x 8 cm.
From the Methodist Modern Art Collection, © TMCP, used with permission.
You can download this image from: www.methodist.org.uk/artcollection

David Jones is most well-known for his 1937 prose poem, *In Parenthesis*, which draws on his World War I experiences. This tiny woodblock was made for a Christmas card while he was living at the Capel-y-ffin community in the Black Mountains of Wales. The local hills feature prominently and below them lies Bethlehem (Carmarthenshire), illuminated by the rays of the star. The words, inscribed in reverse, 'Omnes de Saba Venient' are known from early Epiphany carols and are found in Isaiah 60:6 (NIV): 'All from Sheba will come, bearing gold and incense and proclaiming the praise of the Lord.'

- One of Jones's essays, 'Art and Sacrament', explores the meaning of signs and symbols in everyday life. What might the mutilated tree in the composition mean in the context of the **Worshipping** kings?
- In his writings, Jones argues that the unique ability of human beings to make works of art is a God-like quality. To what extent do you find your own creativity a way of drawing closer to God?
- Seeking Christ in our local setting is a challenge for us all. What helps you to **Worship** God when life seems an uphill struggle?
- Offer everyone a piece of paper and a pencil, and ask them to scribble their picture ideas for what **Worship** means to them. This is not intended to be an art class, more of a way of using visual representation to get us thinking. Discuss what you were seeking to represent with a trusted prayer partner or friend.

Offering

What aspects of **Worship** do you see in this picture? You might look particularly at the hands and the face, as well perhaps at the more obvious features of what is being worn and carried.

The subject of this photo is a child. Does that have any particular significance?

We speak of 'offering worship', but also of a 'service of worship'. Does this photo have anything to say about the language that we use?

Credits

In addition to the Holy Habits editorial/development team, contributions to this booklet also came from: Fiona Beadle, Tina Booker, David Butterworth, Rick Castairs, John Cooper, Christine Dineage, Marjorie Evans, Alison Faulkner, Rachel Frank, Chris Giles, Dorothy Graham, Jean Hamilton, Alex Heagen, Lorna Hewitt, Donal Ker, Tony Malcolm, Sarah Middleton, Grace Milton, Ann Pardoe, James Pollard, Linda Ramdharry, Diane Webb, Caroline Wickens, Georgie Yarnham-Baker and Ruth Yorke.

'This set of ten resources will enable churches and individuals to begin to establish "habits of faithfulness". In the United Reformed Church, we are calling this process of developing discipleship, "Walking the Way: Living the life of Jesus today" and I have no doubt that this comprehensive set of resources will enable us to do just that.'
Revd Richard Church, Deputy General Secretary (Discipleship), United Reformed Church

'Here are some varied and rich resources to help further deepen our discipleship of Christ, encouraging and enabling us to adopt the life-transforming habits that make for following Jesus.'
Revd Dr Martyn Atkins, Team Leader & Superintendent Minister, Methodist Central Hall, Westminster

'The Holy Habits resources will help you, your church, your fellowship group, to engage in a journey of discovery about what it really means to be a disciple today. I know you will be encouraged, challenged and inspired as you read and work your way through each chapter. There is lots to study together and pray about, and that can only be good as our churches today seek to bring about the kingdom of God.'
Revd Loraine Mellor, President of the Methodist Conference 2017/18

'The Holy Habits resources help weave the spiritual through everyday life. They're a great tool that just get better with use. They help us grow in our desire to follow Jesus as their concern is formation not simply information.'
Olive Fleming Drane and John Drane

'The Holy Habits resources are an insightful and comprehensive manual for living in the way of Jesus in the 21st century: an imaginative, faithful and practical gift for the church that will sustain and invigorate our life and mission in a demanding world. The Holy Habits resources are potentially transformational for a church.'
Revd Ian Adams, Mission Spirituality Adviser for Church Mission Society

'To understand the disciplines of the Christian life without practising them habitually is like owning a fine collection of soap but never having a wash. The team behind Holy Habits knows this, which is why they have produced these excellent and practical resources. Use them, and by God's grace you will grow in holiness.'
Paul Bayes, Bishop of Liverpool

'The Holy Habits resources are a rich mine of activities for all ages to help change minds, attitudes and behaviours. I love the way many different people groups are represented and celebrated, and the constant references to the complex realities of 21st-century life.'
Lucy Moore, Founder of BRF's Messy Church